ROYAL BOROUGH OF GREENWICH

Follow us on twitter @greenwichlibs

Please return by the last date shown

Thank you! To renew, please contact any
Royal Greenwich library or renew online or by phone
www.better.org.uk/greenwichlibraries
24hr renewal line **01527 852385**

HIGH STREET LONDINIUM

Reconstructing Roman London

D0807692

H LIBRARIES

3 8028 02296184 8

Cover: Sands Films worker preparing an oak timber for one of the reconstructed Roman interiors
in the Museum of London exhibition, *High Street Londinium.* Photograph by Phil Sayer

Roman London, known as Londinium, must have been an extraordinary place to live. Though positioned at one extremity of the world known to the Romans, hundreds of miles from the Mediterranean heart of their Empire, Londinium's forum and basilica (market and town hall) would be the largest they would build north of the Alps.

Archaeological work over many years has shown that London was located on a previously unoccupied site perfectly placed to facilitate trade and control the new province. Following the Roman invasion of AD43, the army quickly began to lay out roads and buildings to encourage the arrival of foreign merchants and native Britons coming to seek their fortune. It took time, and Londinium in the 1st century AD – the focus of the Museum of London exhibition, *High Street Londinium* – may well have resembled a wild-west frontier town more than familiar images of Rome and Pompeii.

This book tells the story of how the Museum of London took one of the most important excavations of Roman London and used it as the basis for a reconstruction within the Museum called *High Street Londinium*. Between 1994 and 1996, work at 1 Poultry by the Museum of London Archaeology Service uncovered a whole streetplan of buildings, yards, roads, alleys and drains in an excellent state of preservation right at the centre of Roman London. These groundbreaking discoveries have enabled us to reconstruct what it would have been like to live in London at the turn of the second century AD. With the technical expertise of Sands Films, the Museum of London has been able to recreate shops, houses and workshops to enable the visitor to experience Roman life at close quarters.

Right
Walking the *via decumana*. A number of groups specialising in Roman reconstruction helped the Museum of London recreate the feel of an early Roman London 'high street' for one section of the exhibition, *High Street Londinium*.

Roman London

When the Romans first created Londinium, they deliberately chose a site where roads and a bridge could connect to the south across the mud-flats of modern-day Southwark. At high tide the town could be reached by merchant ships that sailed up the Thames laden with commodities from all parts of the Roman Empire.

The site of the main settlement lay north of the Thames, on two steep-sided hills (modern Ludgate Hill and Cornhill) separated by a stream (later called the Walbrook). It was probably planned by military engineers and developed by land speculators and traders wishing to extend their markets. The main area of the early settlement lay to the east of the stream on either side of a main road that ran from east to west. This ribbon development quickly spread westwards across the Walbrook.

Right
Model of the Roman port that stood along the banks of the Thames.

Below
The forum and basilica (market and town hall) would have been the true centre of Roman London.

The early town of around AD50 was built of the area's abundant timber and must have resembled a frontier town more than an imperial city. It only lasted for ten years. British tribes, the Iceni and Trinovantes led by Queen Boudica, burnt the town down, leaving a blackened layer in the archaeological record. The town was soon rebuilt and although domestic shops and houses were made of wood, public buildings were constructed in durable stone and tile. All public buildings were in place or under construction by AD100, by which time Londinium had become the capital of the province of Britannia. This was Roman London at the peak of its prosperity, with public buildings on a grand scale. Yet many of the houses were small and closely packed, fronting onto the main roads that ran through the town. This is the moment in time selected for the Museum's glimpse into Roman London.

The area
excavated
at 1 Poultry

A large area of the town was again destroyed by accidental fire about AD125–135. Little could be done to save the wooden shops and houses. Rebuilding was selective and some areas of the town were left undeveloped. Despite this, Londinium maintained its predominance for the next 300 years, acting as the focal point for a radiating network of land and sea communications for the whole of Roman Britain. The town, although gradually dwindling in size, remained the cosmopolitan centre of administration.

Above
Roman London as it would have looked in AD120. Other visible landmarks include the amphitheatre, fort, forum and basilica, riverfront quays and bridge across the Thames. Painting by Peter Froste.

1 Poultry

The story of the development at 1 Poultry is a long and complex one. It is a key site in the very heart of the City of London, opposite the Bank of England and the Mansion House. Developer Peter Palumbo's longstanding plans to construct a landmark building to replace the street's Victorian buildings were finally approved in 1989, with designs by architect James Stirling. Provision had to be made for the potentially rich archaeology that would be uncovered by the new development. The site's Victorian buildings had shallow foundations and basements and the depth of archaeological levels was likely to be great. Archaeological survival was also likely to be

Right
The new building at 1 Poultry.

Below
The Poultry site is in the heart of the modern City of London.

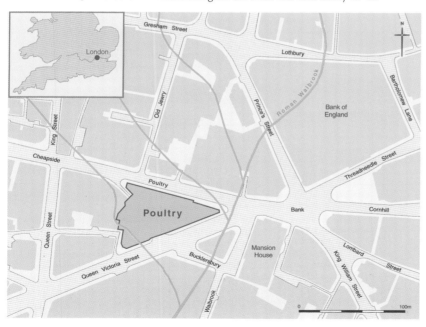

enhanced by the proximity of the Walbrook Valley. The steep banks of the Walbrook stream would provide the waterlogged soil conditions ideal for the preservation of organic material such as wood and leather.

Complex negotiations took place involving English Heritage, the Museum of London and the developers. The solution was to construct the ground floor of the new building initially as a massive concrete platform. The Museum of London Archaeology Service would then have the time it needed to excavate the Roman and later levels underneath while the developers began to construct their new office block above.

The excavation

The excavation at 1 Poultry was one of the largest and most complicated ever undertaken in London. Before work could begin, the limits of the site – both sides bounded major surface roads and underground railway lines – had to be secured by concrete piles. Further piles were sunk into the interior of the site to support the ground-level platform and the floors being built above. This left a massive subterranean space in which the archaeologists could work. Special lighting was set up so archaeologists could clearly identify the complex levels they were uncovering, and an elaborate system allowed trucks in to remove soil that was being excavated. A large multidisciplinary team worked on the site. This included not only highly experienced archaeological excavators but also surveyors, photographers, finds and environmental experts to record the masses of material recovered, and conservators to care for the delicate finds.

It was what it revealed about Roman London that made 1 Poultry so important archaeologically. A major Roman road ran east-west across the site, nine metres wide with large box timber drains running along its edges. Normally referred to as the *via decumana* (the general term for the main east-west road in Roman towns), it was one of the key roads of Roman London, the equivalent of its high street. To the east of the site, the road crossed the Walbrook, facilitating communication between the eastern and the western sides of the town. A series of smaller roads joined the *via decumana* at a major junction in the western part of the site. Shortly after the building of the main road, timber-framed buildings were erected along both sides. After the destruction of early Roman London by Boudica in AD60, the town was rapidly rebuilt, probably with help from the army, and London quickly grew to be a major trading centre. These later buildings – mostly long, thin buildings of mudbrick and timber frames that lined the *via decumana* –

Below
Excavations by the Museum of London Archaeology Service at 1 Poultry.

were a mixture of houses, workshops and shops, in many cases all three at once. Behind them were yards and outhouses. A large tank suggests the use of water in small-scale industrial activity. The area also revealed a mass of broken querns (stones for milling grain), again indicating local industry.

The area remained built up and crowded from the 1st through the 3rd centuries. Traditionally evidence has pointed to a decline in Roman London during the 2nd century AD. At Poultry, however, there is no sign of this. Instead, there is evidence of more substantial stone buildings replacing, or being added to, earlier wooden structures. Only in the later 4th century does the area appear to start falling

into disrepair, a decline symptomatic of the whole town. By the middle of the 5th century, the Roman town had been abandoned.

The site also provided important evidence about later periods of London's history. Cheapside and Poultry remain principal shopping streets in the City, and excavations showed that the area was just as important during the 9th-century Saxon reoccupation of London. In the medieval period, small ironworkers' workshops lined the road prior to the building of large stone residences by wealthier merchants.

timber buildings

terrace line

timber buildings

Via Decumana

limit of excavation

Walbrook

bridge

0   40m

N

The buildings

Timber buildings must have far outnumbered stone structures in Roman Britain. Yet little evidence for Roman timber buildings survives. Some Roman timbers have been found preserved in waterlogged conditions where buildings had been constructed, others in reused contexts. An excavation under Cannon Street Station in 1989 revealed a substantial Roman timber revetment of horizontal timbers constructed on a foundation of oak piles. Some of these timber piles had been reused, and the shaped joints and nailing systems showed that they had originally come from earlier 1st-century buildings. Similar timbers have also been excavated at other sites in the City of London: Bucklersbury, Pudding Lane, Copthall Avenue, Regis House on King William Street and at Suffolk House, adjoining the Cannon Street excavations.

Using the evidence from these timbers, it is now possible for archaeologists to identify differing styles of Roman timber structures from London. In the 1st and 2nd centuries, frames of squared, straight oak timbers were prefabricated and then reassembled on site. They were fitted together to make base-plates, wall-plates and top-plates. The base-plates were laid on the ground with little or no foundation. Vertical corner posts and intermediate studs were jointed into base-plates at intervals of 60cm (2 Roman feet) and diagonal timber braces were fastened to the stud timbers in order to strengthen the frame. Roof structures were added before the walls were completed and tie-beams were inserted to prevent the walls from spreading. The walls may have been as tall as 2.4m and the structures were probably only single-storey. Roofs would have been thatched or made from wooden planks laid either vertically or horizontally. More substantial timber-framed buildings, capable of bearing more weight, may have had tile roofs.

Below
This diagram of a Roman timber-frame building shows how the timber frame was filled in with either mudbrick or wattle and daub before being overlaid with plaster. The window is based on an example excavated at Suffolk House in the City of London.

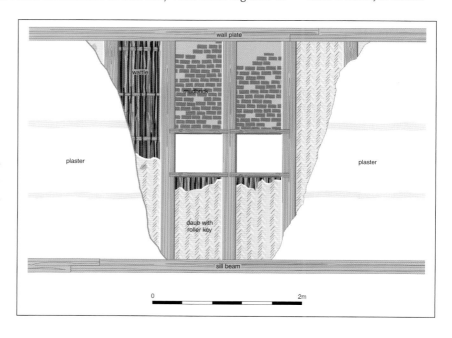

The walls were completed with mudbricks (fashioned earth left to harden) or wattle and daub. To construct the latter, horizontal bars were inserted between the stud timbers, around which pliant wooden rods (laths or withies) were woven. This wattle construction was then covered on both sides by daub, a silty mud-clay. Daub on the upstanding walls was stamped with deep-set chevrons (V-shapes), allowing the plaster rendering to key to the patterned daub. Not all stud timbers were rendered over. Other

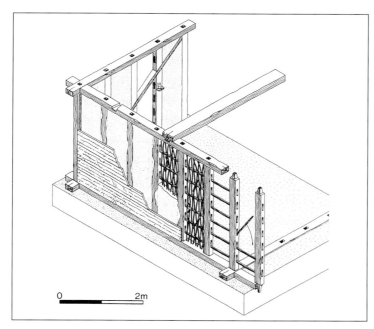

0   2m

examples show that some upright timbers inside rooms were left exposed so that lighting could be attached. An alternative to plaster for weather-proofing the outside of walls, as shown in the Cannon Street timbers, was to clad the walls with horizontal planking.

Although evidence from Roman London can now provide structural information about timber-frame buildings, less is known about windows and doors. The Suffolk House excavations revealed a modified wall with two small window frames inserted between three timber uprights about 1.5m above floor level. A lintel or sill from Poultry appears to have come from a larger mullion window with sockets for a series of upright bars. Although a corner segment of a panelled internal door had been previously excavated from Regis House, the most complete Roman door yet from London was found during the Poultry excavation.

The High Street Londinium experiment

The evidence from 1 Poultry, enhanced by information from other sites, has provided the first opportunity actually to reconstruct Roman London's timber-framed buildings. This is what the Museum of London has done for its *High Street Londinium* exhibition. The exact plans of three buildings from the northern side of the *via decumana* have been followed. Two of them, a bakery and a craftworker's house, are as they may have looked in AD100, and another, a merchant's shop, as it was before being destroyed in the Boudican fire of AD60.

The site for the bakery was prepared by cutting a terrace into the downward slope of the Walbrook valley. Some of the walls survived to a height of 25–30cm. No timber uprights survived, but two timber plank thresholds remained, one external and one internal, indicating the width of the doorways. An external hearth made from deliberately broken fragments of flat clay tiles had been built into the building's back wall. This oven opened onto a large area behind,

Left
Artist's impression of part of Roman London in AD100, based on the Poultry excavations. The *High Street Londinium* buildings are on the north side of the *via decumana* (bottom right). Painting by Judith Dobie. Reproduced by permission of English Heritage.

where bread ovens and numerous fragments of quernstones and millstones were excavated. In rubbish dumps around the building, fragments of wooden dough troughs and oven waste were also found.

By AD100 the bakery had existed for 30 years, longer than is usual for this type of building. The reconstruction is of a weathered building that has seen better days. It has a front shop, where freshly-baked bread is sold, and rooms on either side of a central corridor, one for preparing and the other for serving food – in effect, a Roman café or tavern. Small mullion windows are set high under the eaves of the outside walls, and although the roof space is open, revealing the massive oak rafters, little natural light can have reached into the rooms. Candles would have been the most likely form of lighting.

The house of the craftworker (probably a carpenter) was separated from the neighbouring bakery by an overgrown alley. This house was a narrow strip building with three rooms running from front to back and a long corridor along the western side. A lean-to had been added at the back. In the back yard, the base-plates of an outhouse, which may have held the family's livestock, also survived.

Above left
One of the reconstructed mullion windows.

Below left
Oak-framed wall being built in preparation for the *High Street Londinium* exhibition.

Above right
Quernstones, used for milling grain, excavated at 1 Poultry.

In the reconstruction, the front room of the dwelling is a shop, while the family use the central room as an all-purpose kitchen, living room and bedroom. The L-shaped back room is the carpenter's workshop, where the mullion windows are based on evidence from elsewhere on the site. The living room has a small glazed window to let in light but not air. There is a hearth built in a hollow in the brickearth floor and smoke from its fire must have escaped through the roof. A tiled surface beside it acts as a hot-plate, while another hollow is full of food waste. Environmental archaeologists have identified the surviving bones of sheep, chicken and thrush, and fishbones of herring, eel, plaice, smelt and thornback ray. Examples of pips and seeds, carefully retrieved by sieving, show that the family were consuming locally grown and imported foods, including sloes, plums, blackberries and hazelnuts.

The merchant's shop shared a narrow alley with the neighbouring building (the forerunner to the craftworker's house) and a communal gutter that channelled rainwater from the roofs of both buildings into the main drain that ran along the road. It was a long strip building with a shop fronting onto the road, two further rooms behind and a corridor running from front to back on the eastern side. Here daub walls survived to a height of 50cm. There was no sill at the front of the building, indicating that there may have been removable wooden shutters that opened the shop to customers. The faces of the daub walls were stamped with a chevron pattern to help key the plaster, no trace of which remained. In the back room, a well made from a reused wooden barrel had been sunk into the brickearth floor.

Below
A preference for beef was part of the Romanised diet. These cattle bones have been chopped into joints of meat.

Bottom of page
Burnt remains of some of the decorated pottery bowls that formed the stock of the merchant's shop, destroyed in the fire of AD60.

13

The life of this new building was cut short in AD60. Surviving fragments showed that the shop and central stockroom had been stocked with glossy red samian and olive-green glazed vessels imported from France. Fire had caused the shop's wooden shelves to collapse, and wooden and bone spoons were found on the floor mixed with wooden beads and imported spices. The nature of his stock indicates a merchant wealthy enough to finance trade in these expensive tablewares, wealthy at least until his business was destroyed in Queen Boudica's rebellion.

Actually reconstructing the buildings uncovered at 1 Poultry, instead of just studying them as archaeological remains, gives us a fascinating insight into the life of 1st century AD Londoners. These buildings would have been relatively cramped, dark and damp. Wells were dug into floors and hearths for cooking and heating stood open in the middle of the room. Living conditions would have been no more than basic. However the buildings were well constructed and functional. They would have performed their task of providing working, trading and living space for a population newly established in this Roman town.

Conclusion

Most of us were taught about the Romans at school. We are surrounded by buildings based on classical architecture, visit Roman monuments and have seen films and television programmes about Roman history. Yet archaeology has demonstrated that this familiar picture of the Roman world differs greatly from reality. Excavations at 1 Poultry showed that 1st-century Roman London was not populated by senators going to the forum or the baths in flowing togas. Nor was it full of stone columns and marble façades. The buildings of early Roman London were made of timber, mudbrick and wattle and daub, their floors of flattened earth. Buildings doubled as homes, workshops and shops, and were probably mass-produced, production-line carpentry replacing the work of single craftsmen.

The imperial veneer of Roman London would have been thin. Roman soldiers would have spent more time constructing roads and buildings or as civil servants than as fighting men. These few governed a broad mix of foreign merchants, businessmen and craftsmen keen to profit from the new province and native Britons only one or two generations removed from their rural origins. London would have been a settlement of many languages, many races, many beliefs, many ways of life. This 'town' was a new concept in Britain, bringing disparate groups together with a variety of social, cultural and economic ambitions. The town became a place of profit and exploitation, but also one where problems were solved, new and dynamic cultures developed and people learned to live together. Roman London would have been unhealthy, smelly, crowded and no doubt at times very dangerous. It would also have been an exciting and dramatic first stage in the history of a city that would survive the decline of the Roman Empire and rise again.

Below
How Roman was Roman London? Although Londinium was a very Roman creation and evidence for Roman society and culture is strong, *High Street Londinium*'s aim was to challenge our preconceptions by using archaeological evidence to reconstruct a city of wooden buildings and mud floors.

Acknowledgements

The Museum of London excavations at 1 Poultry were funded by Lord Palumbo/City Acre Property Invesment Trust in a joint venture with Advanta. Project management was by Altstadtbau. The post-excavation analysis was funded by English Heritage. Excavations were undertaken by the Museum of London Archaeology Service (MoLAS). Post-excavation work was undertaken by MoLAS and the Museum of London Specialist Services. The *High Street Londinium* exhibition was sponsored by Banca di Roma. Construction of the exhibition was by Sands Films. We are grateful to English Heritage and MoLAS for the use of photographs, maps and paintings. The authors are also grateful to the following for help in compiling this book: Peter Rowsome, Julian Hill, Damian Goodburn.

Of further interest

Heart of the City
Roman, medieval and modern London revealed at 1 Poultry
by Peter Rowsome
(Museum of London Archaeology Service, 2000)

This book provides a fuller account of the remarkable archaeological dig at 1 Poultry, a site at the heart of London for the last 2000 years. In the 1990s, hidden from public view, a team of archaeologists uncovered mosaics, timber and stone buildings, and thousands of coins, pots and other objects. The finds tell the story of London – from rural idyll to Roman frontier town; ruin then revival as medieval Europe's largest city; recovery from fire and plague to become the world's richest metropolis.

Heart of the City tells of the discoveries made and, with specially commissioned reconstructions, brings the past to life for anyone interested in archaeology, history, architecture, or simply in London.

Back cover: Recreating a Roman London roof at Sands Films in preparation for the exhibition, *High Street Londinium*.